A Christmas Story

A Christmas Story

Richard Burton

Introduction by Sally Burton

Hodder & Stoughton

LONDON SYDNEY AUCKLAND TORONTO

British Library Cataloguing in Publication Data
Burton, Richard, *1925-1984*
   A Christmas Story
   I. Title
   823'.914 [F]

   ISBN 0-340-51246 6

This edition first published in Great Britain 1989
Second Impression 1989

Book designed by L. Back

Published by Hodder and Stoughton,
a division of Hodder and Stoughton Ltd,
Mill Road, Dunton Green, Sevenoaks, Kent TN13 2YA
Editorial Office: 47 Bedford Square, London WC1B 3DP

Photoset by BWS Graphics, London

Printed in Great Britain by St. Edmundsbury Press Ltd.,
Bury St. Edmunds, Suffolk

A
Christmas
Story

Introduction
by Sally Burton

To imagine that Richard Burton had an impoverished childhood is to fall too readily into a foolish trap. The facts remain the same: born November 10th, 1925 in Pontrydyfen, the twelfth son of thirteen children, two of whom died in infancy, father a sometime miner who liked a drink or two, a mother who died five days after giving birth to her thirteenth child, another boy, taken in by an elder sister, his beloved Cis, and finally 'adopted' by Philip Burton. It is the interpretation that changes. From a distance of over fifty years it is all too easy to place those facts against a backdrop of the effects of the Depression, pit villages with grey terraced houses, high unemployment with whatever jobs there were available being backbreaking work down the mines, where fearsome accidents were always a possibility, women working themselves to the bone to feed their families and keep the house clean, the diseases derived from an inadequate diet and a lifetime hammering at the coalface, and come to the conclusion that the Jenkins family must have been abject and poverty stricken. Wrong.

Lacking in funds they might have been, with a father who was at best imprudent, stretched to the limit they most certainly were with a fast growing family of demanding sturdy children to take care of and feed. But there were other things going on. Gripped in adversity as they were, there was always a strong emphasis on the family unit, of looking after your own, of education, getting on in life and, if you could not move on yourself, making sure those who followed you could, and at least doing what you have to do to the best of your ability. It was a case of 'meet your lot head on and don't give in'. Those were feelings which were true not only for the Jenkins family but were held up as mainstays throughout the valleys. With those values firmly in position it was a good place to start.

But let us not get too carried away with the romance of it all and start to imagine it with a Hollywood sound track. In 1921 there was a miners' strike which lasted three months and in 1926 a strike which was to last a long and bitter six months. From the mid-twenties through until the mid-thirties the effects of the Depression bit with unrelenting hardness and without discrimination. English towns did

Edith, his mother, who died when Rich was two, and his father, known as Dic Bach.

Rich as a baby.

their bit by adopting Welsh pit villages, collecting much needed money to provide soup kitchens in the schools and sending old clothes which were distributed amongst the most needy. The slow drift of migration, to London and the industrial Midlands, began in the vain hope of finding jobs and an alternative living. Hardship was rife in the valleys.

As for the Jenkins family, they kept themselves together and much credit for that must go to their mother, Edith, who was thought by many to be an absolute angel. She was one of those strong Welsh women imbued with natural pride and dignity, determination and a vast range of practical talents. There were a lot of them and there still are today. To this day her seventh child, David Jenkins, speaks of her extraordinary ability in keeping family and home together against all odds. She worked unceasingly. He talks of the massive meals she prepared for them all, sitting her huge family around the kitchen table – it is her baking of the pies made from the wimberries which grew wild in the nearby hills that he remembers best. It is a marvel how she, with the help of her eldest daughter Cis, did it. Quite obviously the work load was enormous but there was never any lowering of standards; the house always shone, there was always enough to eat, the children were well turned out and the washing never ceased. Even with that burden apparently she found time for all her children, each of them different, each of them talented in their varying ways.

Their father, Dic Bach, had a bit of the devil in him, he was a character, he told stories and he made them laugh. The children knew from an early age that he was not always going to be there for them, that he was unreliable, but he was their father and they loved him all the

Rich with his brother-in-law Elfed, Auntie Ethel and cousin Dilwyn.

same. He was a bit different from the rest, he read books, he liked to play with long words and he had opinions which he was all too happy to expound. Their mother was their rock, she was beautiful, she was their inspiration and was the one who would always be there to come home to. Five days after giving birth to her thirteenth child she died.

The loss of their mother devastated the family and Dic Bach who had worshipped her would never be the same. They say he never looked at another woman. The impact of her death upon the family was enormous. For a start there were all those children to be looked after – Tom and Cis were married – but at home there was Ifor who would take control, Will, Verdun, David, Hilda, Edie, Cassie, Rich, and the new baby. But first things first. It was decided that Tom would take Graham, the baby, and Cis would take Rich aged two, a hefty and lively little boy who used to cry whenever his mother left him. It was a decision made without hesitation for Cis, though it was probably very difficult for her husband, Elfed, to accept as he had been told by her that she did not want to have children of her own. He hoped she would change her mind, which in time she did, but then she felt she had had quite enough of children at home where she had helped her mother take care of the regularly growing family. Cis had de-spaired for her mother as she watched her wear herself out and at times she actively disliked her father for it. Babies, babies and more babies. Work, work, and more work. Cis had never really received a proper education because of relentless demands of home and children.

So Rich was taken from the secure world of Pontrydyfen to the unknown territory of Caradoc Street, Taibach, a few miles down the road. Now only a few minutes in a car but then, if you happened to be two and spoke only in Welsh, the distance was monumental. Cis and Rich travelled that distance time and time again. Sometimes quite unknown to Elfed. Edith had handed down her housekeeping skills to Cis who now used them in her own house and at the family home in Pontrydyfen. To and fro they went, with an old suitcase full of washing, collecting and delivering. One time the catch broke and the much used suitcase burst open in front of a bus queue. Cis and Rich had to get down on their knees and struggle to gather up the washing and force the case shut again – oh the shame of it. Because Elfed was concerned that Cis was taking on too much in attempting to run two homes, the frequency of the journeys had to be kept a secret from him. From an early age Cis and Rich were locked in a conspiracy of secrecy and total adoration.

Though Cis had worried for her mother having all those babies, from the moment he was born there was no doubt that she was utterly devoted to Rich whom she thought the most beautiful baby she had ever seen. Brother Ifor was more dismissive of the latest addition to the family but soon even he was captivated by this engaging child who seemed to have something undefinable but very powerful about him. If the other children spotted Ifor coming home from work with a sullen

Cecilia, known to the family as Cis. 'I shone in the reflection of her green-eyed, black-haired, gypsy beauty.'

Rich as a boy.

expression and clearly in a bad mood which they were going to get the sharp end of, Rich would instantly be popped up on top of the kitchen table and told to dance. In later life he had no sense of rhythm at all so it is not hard to understand why Ifor would burst out in uncontrollable laughter at the hilarious sight of those fat little legs attempting a charleston.

In Taibach Rich quickly picked up English and it seems he managed with his reading just as well. He said he could not remember learning to read, that he just seemed to be able to do it. There was no struggling with the alphabet or tracing a finger along lines of indecipherable words for him. The next door neighbour in Caradoc Street used to pass on her weekly magazine to Cis and while she was busy doing the ironing, of which there was always a mountain, Rich would entertain her by reading the stories. So it would seem that the great Burton voice got its first airing reading romantic fiction from women's magazines to the accompaniment of an iron swishing back and forth, back and forth.

Other talents also started to emerge. Rich loved to imitate. The local preachers were some of his first victims and so was Elfed. Rich could do his walk and made quite a fuss about having a coat and a cap just like him. Cis even had to find a junior version of Elfed's pipe so that the budding star could do the full affectionate portrayal.

He had his friends. There was Trevor from next door and there was his cousin Dilwyn, and together the three fearlessly roamed Taibach and the surrounding area. Nearby they had the sea where they could swim — with the passage of time Rich became convinced that they did it in all weathers, endowing the Gulf Stream and the intrepid hardiness of children with all kinds of extraordinary powers. Brother Verdun came up trumps by building the best boneshaker ever. It impressed the hell out of the other boys and was immediately put into service up and down Caradoc Street. There were all kinds of aunts and uncles and, if they were not all strictly related, they were given the honorary title which came to the same thing. With this huge network of admirers Rich could come and go as he pleased, always assured of a welcome. Front doors were left open and there were usually a couple of pennies here, and a couple more there, to be earned or just be given out of pure generosity as Rich developed his certain way with people.

Over the years Rich continued to shuttle between Taibach and Pontrydyfen. While the house in Caradoc Street was his home, he spent weekends with his other brothers and sisters in the house he had been born in at 2 Dan-y-Bont, Pontrydyfen. There he would share beds and listen late at night to his sisters giggling while telling each other of their romantic outings, particularly one who had

met the man of her dreams who lived only streets away and looked 'just like Robert Taylor'.

Home life was good, school life was good; though Rich began to strain at the leash a bit as an adolescent. He was a strong and very bright boy who was finding the confines of Taibach frustrating, though at that time he could not define why and certainly did not know how to express his doubts other than by being ill-tempered and difficult. No more so than most teenagers. It was thought that he needed the discipline of a job, and anyway he should begin to pay his way, so he was yanked out of school and given the all-consuming task of working in the haberdashery department of the local co-op. It was not an easy relationship.

Fortunately Rich was rescued, returned to school, and put on a surer route. He was able to follow that direction and see wherever it would take him because he had those strong roots forged in his Welsh childhood with Cis. It took him into an uncharted world which he conquered with tremendous success, inspiring enormous pride amongst his own family, and the greater family of Wales. He fulfilled his own and their dreams. Rich had a mighty range of talents, many ambitions, and one of them was to write. A short piece, *A Christmas Story*, was first published in 1964. During that year he played Hamlet in New York, and made the films *Becket* in London and *Night of the Iguana* in Mexico, but for this short story he returned to his childhood to pay tribute to Cis and to Wales.

If the theory that all men are really little boys at heart is true, and to those who knew him Rich was more than most men, then it follows that he was even more of a little boy. There were certainly times when he was mischievous – he got himself into the odd scrape or two, the effects of which resounded much further than Port Talbot – but he also had a sense of adventure and a desire to try anything for size. There was always a feeling of what stunt could he invent next, what prank could he get up to. He saw the world through his own eyes, and he was a joy to be around. After his death in 1984 I was asked if I regretted not having a child. My response was that I had one, a little boy, he was fifty-eight years old.

Sally Burton
London, 1989

———————◆ ◆———————

I am extremely grateful to Hilda Owen for the loan of pictures from the Jenkins family albums reproduced on pages 12, 14, 16 and 17. Glyn Thomas kindly lent me the photograph on page 13 and was always available with information. The school rugby team photograph on page 52 was one of Rich's own proud possessions and he is readily recognisable seated second from the right in the second row.

The other photographs, many from Pontrhydyfen, Taibach and the surrounding villages in the 1920s and 1930s, speak too eloquently for themselves to need captions. I should like to thank my friend Annette Balfour-Lynn for finding them. Their sources are acknowledged on page 60.

My grateful thanks also go to Ion Trewin for his encouragement and to Margaret Body for her gentle insight.

S.B.

A Christmas Story

❦

THERE WERE NOT many white Christmases in our part of Wales in my childhood – perhaps only one or two – but Christmas cards and Dickens and Dylan Thomas and wishful memory have turned them all into white. I don't know why there should have been so few in such a cold, wet land – the nearness of the sea, perhaps. The Atlantic, by way of the Bristol Channel, endlessly harried us with gale and tempest. Perhaps our winds were too wild and salty for the snow to get a grip. Perhaps they blew the snow over us to the Black Mountains and Snowdonia and England.

Most of the Christmases of my childhood seem the same, but one of them I remember particularly, because it departed from the seemingly inexorable ritual. On this Eve of Christmas, Mad Dan, my uncle, the local agnostic, feared for his belief but revered for his brilliantly active vocabulary in the half-alien English tongue, sat in our kitchen with a group of men and with biting scourge and pithy whip drove the great cries of history, the epoch-making, world-changing ones, out of the the temple of time. They were all half-truths, he said, and therefore half-lies.

I sat and stoned raisins for the pudding and listened bewitched to this exotic foreign language, this rough and r-riddled, rolling multisyllabic English.

'"There is only one Christian and he died upon the Cross," said Nietzsche,' said Dan.

Nietzsche, I thought – a Japanese. Perhaps he can speak Japanese, I thought. It was said that he, Dan, knew Latin and Greek, and could write both of them backwards.

'Can you speak Japanese, Mad Dan?' I asked.

'Shut up, Solomon,' he said to me.

'"Workers of the world, unite! You have nothing to lose but your chains,"' he said. 'Irresponsible rubbish. Cries written by crabbed fists on empty tables from mean hearts.

'" *Dulce et decorum est pro patria mori.*"'

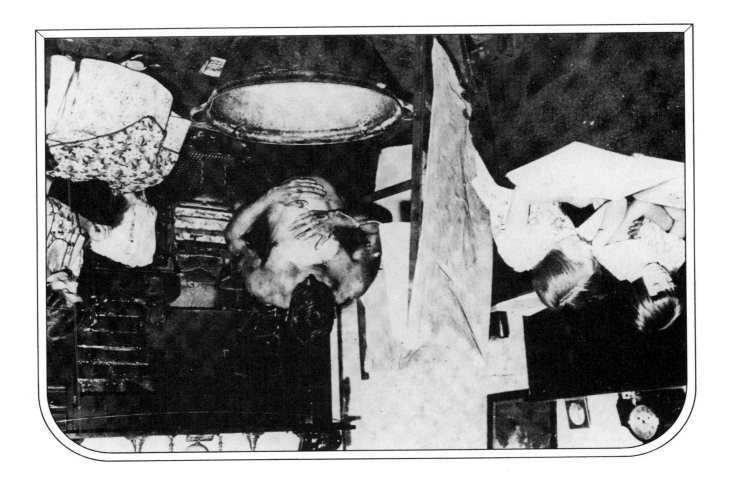

'What's that?' I asked.

'Latin, Copperfield,' he said, 'meaning it is sweetly bloody marvellous to die for your country.

'"Man is born free and is everywhere in chains" – golden-tongued, light-brained, heedlessness of consequences.

'"I think, therefore I am" – Descartes.'

'French,' I guessed.

'Right, Seth,' he said. 'Thou shalt have a Rolls-Royce and go to Oxford and never read a book again.

'"I think, therefore I am,"' with scorn. 'Wallace the fruiterer – he who sells perishable goods after they have perished to Saturday night idiots – might well say of them, "They do not think, therefore they are not, they buy perishable goods after they have perished."'

Out of the welter of names and quotations (Mad Dan's 'My personal leaden treasury of the human tragedy') the cries, the references rolled out endlessly. He said that Martin Luther should have had a diet of worms. Why, I thought, why should the man eat worms?

'Can you eat worms?' I asked.

'Not as readily as the worms will eat you,' he said. He roared with delight at this incomprehensible joke. He had become more and more burning and bright. He said he had a cold, and took some more medicine from a little bottle in his pocket.

This was as it should be. Uncle Dan had been talking ever since I could remember. Until this moment Christmas was Christmas as it always had been. But then my sister's husband, cheekboned, hollowed, sculpted, came into the room.

'All right, boys,' he said, 'off you go – take the boy with you.'

'Where to?' I asked.

'Just go with Dan and behave yourself,' he said.

'Where's my sister?' I said.

'Never mind,' he said. 'Go you.'

I went out into the night with Dan and the other men.

Why were they sending me out at this time of night on

PONTRHYDYFEN

Christmas Eve?

My mother had died when I was two years old, and I had lived with my sister and her husband ever since. I had had lots of Christmases since my mother's death, and they could already be relied on, they had always been the same. There was the growing excitement of Uncle Ben's Christmas Club (you paid a sixpence or shilling a week throughout the year), and the choosing from the catalogue – *Littlewood's Catalogue*. There was the breathless guessing at what Santa Claus would bring. What was in those anonymous brown paper parcels on top of the wardrobe? Would it be a farm with pigs in a sty, and ducks on a metal pond, and five-barred gates and metal trees, and Kentucky fences, and a horse or two, and several cows, and a tiny bucket and a milk-maid, and a farmhouse complete with red-faced farmer and wife in the window? And a chimney on top? Pray God it wasn't Tommy Elliot's farm, which I'd played with for two years and which I feared – from glances and whispers that I'd caught between my sister and Mrs. Elliot – was going to be cleaned up and bought for me for Christmas. It would be shameful to have a secondhand present. Everybody would know. It must be, if a farm at all, a spanking-new one, gleaming with fresh paint, with not a sign of the leaden base showing through.

And I would spend an hour singing Christmas carol duets from door to door with my friend Trevor, picking up a penny here and a ha'penny there. And then home at nine o'clock, perhaps to gossip with my sister and eat more nuts, and be sent to bed sleepless and agog. And now, at the time of getting to bed, I was being sent out into the night with Mad Dan and his audience – all of them with Christmas colds, and all of them drinking medicine out of little bottles kept in their inside pockets.

We went to the meeting ground of our part of the village. It was called 'The End'. It was a vacant stretch of stony ground between two rows of cottages – Inkerman and Balaclava. Both the Inkerman people and the Balaclava people called it 'The End'. Insularity, I realize now,

streetophobia – to each street it was 'The End'. It should have been called 'The Middle'.

The miners had built a bonfire and stood around it, burning on one side and frozen on the other. Chestnuts and – because there had been plenty of work that year – potatoes were roasted to blackness, and eaten sprinkled with salt, smoky and steaming straight from the fire. And Mad Dan, making great gestures against the flames, told the half-listening, silent, munching miners of the lies we had been told for thousands of years, the mellifluous advice we had been told to take.

'Turn the other cheek. Turn the other cheek, boys, and get your bloody brain broken. Suffer all my children. This side of the river is torment and torture and starvation, and don't forget the sycophancy to the carriaged and horsed, the Daimlered, the bare-shouldered, remote beauties in many mansions, gleaming with the gold we made for them. Suffer all my baby-men, beat out, with great coal-hands, the black melancholy of the hymns. When you die and cross that stormy river, that roaring, Jordan, there will be un-imaginable delights, and God shall wipe away all tears, and there will be no more pain. Lies! Lies! Lies!'

The night was getting on. Christmas was nearly here. Dan was boring now, and sometimes he didn't make sense, and he was repeating himself. What was in those parcels on top of the wardrobe, and why had I been sent out so late on Christmas Eve? I wanted to go home.

'Can I go home now, Mad Dan?'

'Shut your bloody trap and listen,' he said, 'or I'll have you apprenticed to a haberdasher.'

This was a fate worse than death for a miner's son. There was, you understand, the ambition for the walk of the miners in corduroy trousers, with yorks under the knees to stop the loose coal running down into your boots and the rats from running up inside your trousers and biting your belly (or worse), and the lamp in the cap on the head, and the bandy, muscle-bound strut of the lords of the coalface. There was the ambition to be one of those blue-scarred boys at the street

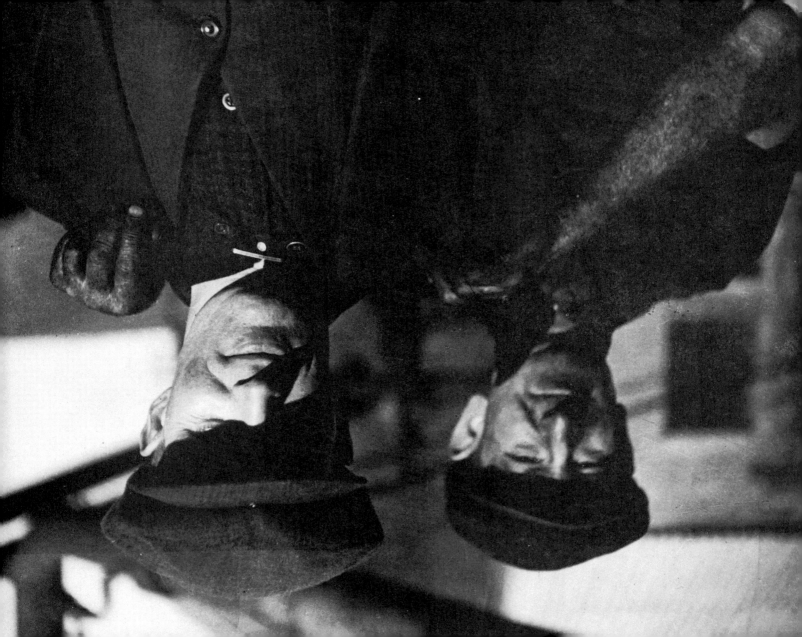

Railway Station, Pontrhydyfen, Nr Neath

corner on Saturday night with a half a crown in the pocket and, secure in numbers, whistle at the girls who lived in the residential area. The doctor's, the lawyer's, the headmaster's daughter.

And Dan roared on. He said he believed nothing and believed everything. That he knew nothing and knew everything. He said that he was the Voltaire of Aberavon. He wept once or twice, and the silent miners chewed and stared uneasily. Crying was for women, or for preachers when talking of God's magnanimity, his mercy, his love. Miners did not weep – not even gabby miners like Mad Dan, who evaded work whenever he could. Mad Dan, with passionate eloquence, had long been an advocate of frequent and lasting strikes. Life was too rough to cry about.

I tried to sneak out of the circle around the bonfire and make my way home, but one of the miners caught me by the ear and brought me painfully back. 'You'll go home when we go home,' he said.

Dan didn't *speak* any more – he chuntered on – that is to

say he would have been mumbling into his beard, had he had a beard. There came out of the grey embers of his dying oratory occasional flashes of coherence.

'Who sent the slave back to his master?'

'Was St. Paul a Christian?'

And, with snarling sarcasm, 'There was an Israelite indeed in whom there was much guile.'

'"Give me liberty or give me death."'

'"Thou has conquered, O pale Galilean; the world has grown grey from thy breath."'

The wind, tigerish, now crouched, now circled, now menaced the bonfire. And the bonfire, now rearing back from, now roaring back at the wind, would send showers of sparks and smoke and coloured flame up the endless open chimney of the night. I was bored and bewildered. I pondered on some of the half-baked things that Uncle Mad Dan had been saying – he talked like a book, they said of him. What did Mad Dan mean about cries being lies? Anyway, his cries didn't sound much like cries to me. They sounded

like sentences. Cries were screams and things like that when somebody twisted your arm or busted your nose. How could 'Turn the other cheek' be a cry? Or 'God is love' or 'The wages of sin is death'? I dimly guessed what time in mist confounds. Why was the Twenty-third Psalm a poem of incomparable beauty? The teacher in school had said it was. I puzzled about this, too. It didn't rhyme. How could it be a poem if it didn't rhyme?

What were cries? How could something be a half-truth? Why were cries lies? Why couldn't I go home? Why was I kept out so late on Christmas Eve, when Holy Santa was due any time after midnight? I dimly guessed what time in mist confounds.

Why had my sister been upstairs all this night on Christmas Eve when I was home? Why wasn't she peeling potatoes, or something? Why were two of my aunties sitting in the parlour, and with them Mrs. Tabor T.B. – she who wore her husband's cap on back to front? Why did they talk low? I dimly guessed. Was my sister dead? Dying? I loved my sister – sometimes with an unbearable passion.

I suddenly knew that she was dying.

'Is my sister dying, Mad Dan?' I said.

'We are all dying, Nebuchadnezzar,' he said.

'Even your growing pains are reaching into oblivion. She'll last the night, Dyfrig,' he said. 'She'll last the night.'

Now my sister was no ordinary woman – no woman ever is, but to me, my sister less than any. When my mother had died, she, my sister, had become my mother, and more mother to me than any mother could ever have been. I was immensely proud of her. I shone in the reflection of her green-eyed, black-haired, gypsy beauty. She sang at her work in a voice so pure that the local men said she had a bell in every tooth, and was gifted by God. And these pundits who revelled in music of any kind and who had agreed many times, with much self-congratulations, that of all instruments devised by man, crwth, violin, pibcorn, dulcimer, viola, church organ, zither, harp, brass band, woodwind, or symphony orchestra – they had smugly agreed that there was no noise as beautiful at its best as the sound of the human voice.

Old Mill, Cymmer. 883

She had a throat that should have been coloured with down like a small bird, and eyes so hazel-green and open that, to preserve them from too much knowledge of evil, should have been hooded and vultured and not, as they were, terrible in their vulnerability. She was innocent and guileless and infinitely protectable. She was naïve to the point of saintliness, and wept a lot at the misery of others. She felt all tragedies except her own. I had read of the Knights of Chivalry and I knew that I had a bounden duty to protect her above all other creatures. It wasn't until thirty years later, when I saw her in another woman, that I realised I had been searching for her all my life.

Why had I been sent out? When would they let me go home? Why were my aunties there, and Mrs. Tabor T.B.? (She was called Mrs. Tabor T.B. because she'd had eight children, all of whom had died in their teens of tuberculosis. She was slightly mad, I think, and would mutter to herself, 'It wasn't Jack or me. T.B. was in the walls. The Council should have had that house fumigated. The T.B. was in the walls.')

Mad Dan was silent now. His stoned eyes stared into the fire. A little spittle guttered quietly from the corner of his mouth.

'Let's have a song, boys,' he said slowly. 'Stay me with minims, comfort me with crotchets.'

The crag-faced miners sang with astonishing sweetness a song about a little engine.

> 'Crawshaw Bailey had an engine;
> It was full of mighty power.
> He was pull little lever;
> It was go five miles an hour.
> Was you ever see,
> Was you ever see,
> Was you ever see
> Such a funny thing before?'

They sang a hymn about what you could see from the hills of Jerusalem; they sang a song about a saucepan – of a green

River Afan, Pontrhydyfen.   No. 16.

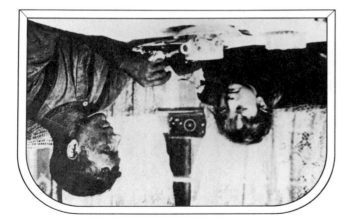

hill far away, without a city wall; of a black pig and how necessary and how dreadful it was to kill it; of the Shepherds and the Magi. Mad Dan stared, and I sang soprano.

There was a disturbance outside the fire's night wall and my Auntie Jinnie came suddenly into the light. Mad Dan stood up.

'All right?' he said.

'Lovely,' she said. 'Nine pounds – a wench.'

'Come, Joseph of Arimathea,' he said to me. 'Santa called early tonight. Home we go.'

We walked a few steps.

'Oh!' he said. 'Any of you boys got a piece of silver? A tanner would do, but half a crown or a florin would be tidier.'

One of the men threw him a florin. 'Tell her it's a happy Christmas from Nat Williams, and all that,' he said.

We went home. Mrs. Tabor T.B. was downstairs in the kitchen, husband's cap on back to front. My brother-in-law was whistling at the hearth, with the flat iron and the nuts, working steadily. My Auntie Jinnie and my Auntie Cassie,

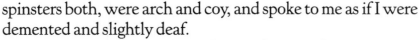

spinsters both, were arch and coy, and spoke to me as if I were demented and slightly deaf.

'Santy Clausie has brought Richie-Pitchie a prezzy-wezzy for Christmas. Go upstairs and see what Santy has brought you.'

I went upstairs with Mad Dan. As I went, Mrs. Tabor T.B. said to my breath-whistling, nut-cracking brother-in-law, 'Talk to the Council, Elfed,' she said, 'get them to fumigate the whole house.'

I dimly guessed, of course, but there was still a chance that there would be a fire engine, loud-red and big enough for an eight-year-old to ride in. The prezzy-wezzy was a furious, red-faced, bald, wrinkled old woman, sixty minutes old.

'Try this for size,' said Mad Dan, and pressed the florin into the baby's left hand. She held the money tightly. 'You've got a good grip,' said Mad Dan to the baby. 'She'll never be poor,' he said to my sister.

My sister looked washed-out and weak. She smiled at me, and I gave her a kiss.

'Well, what do you think of your Christmas present?' she said.

'Fine,' I said. 'Is this all I get?'

'No, there'll be more in the morning.'

'O.K.,' I said. 'Good night, then.'

We went downstairs together, and the baby screamed.

'There,' said Mad Dan, 'is the only cry that is true and immortal and eternal and from the heart. Screaming we come into the world and screaming we go out.'

'Well, what do you think of your new sister?' they asked in the kitchen.

'New *niece*,' I said. 'Fine.'

I went to my bed in the boxroom. The bed was old, and the springs had long ago given up, and sleeping in it was like sleeping in a hammock.

My brother-in-law blew out the candle. 'Sleep now,' he said. 'No lighting the candle and reading.' He closed the door and went downstairs.

I pulled the clothes over my head, made a tent, felt for my

Woolworth's torch, and with *John Halifax, Gentleman* propped against my knees, began to read. The Atlantic wind, wild from America, whooped and whistled around the house. The baby choked with sobs on the other side of the bedroom wall. I listened. Well, at least, I thought, it isn't Tommy Elliot's farm.

Picture credits

The main jacket photograph of the Afan valley under snow is reproduced by permission of the Welsh Miners Museum, and the inset portrait of Richard Burton by permission of Camera Press Ltd.

Sally Burton and the publishers are also grateful to the following copyright-holders for the loan of their photographs:

John Cornwall Archive: pp 10, 45 (below left).

Edith Tudor Hart (© W. Suschitzky): pp 26, 29 (right), 37, 41 (left), 49, 55, 56.

Hulton Picture Library: p 42.

National Museum of Wales: pp 25, 45 (above right).

Popperfoto: p 59.

Port Talbot Historical Society: pp 34 (left), 45 (below right).

Arthur Rees: p 19.

Welsh Miners Museum: pp 22, 29 (left), 30, 33, 34 (right), 38, 41 (right), 45 (above left), 46, 51 (all four pictures), and the endpaper.